Totally Amazing
Careers in
AEROSPACE

Sally Ride
Science

CONTENTS

Dava

Michael

Ephrahim

Janice

Lorenda

Alexandre

Aprille

Victoria

Penny

MECHANICAL ENGINEER

MISSION DESIGNER

NAVIGATION ENGINEER

Christopher

PSYCHOLOGIST

Jananda

SOFTWARE ENGINEER

SPACE HISTORIAN

Roger

ABOUT ME

What Do You Want To Be?

It's never too soon to think about what you want to be.

You probably have lots of things that you like to do—maybe you like doing experiments or drawing pictures. Or maybe you like working with numbers or writing stories.

Is working in aerospace one of your goals? The good news is that there are many different areas to focus on. The people in aerospace work on everything from rockets, computers, and airplanes to satellites, spacecraft, and even study natural fliers, such as birds and insects.

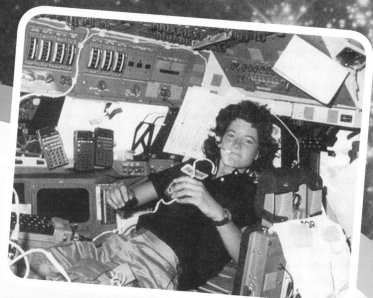

SALLY RIDE
First American Woman in Space

The women and men you're about to meet found their careers by doing what they love. As you read this book and do the activities, think about what you like doing. Then follow your interests and see where they take you. You just might find your career, too. Reach for the stars!

Sally K. Ride

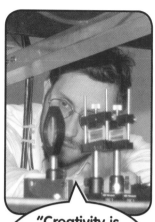

"Creativity is always required in problem solving."

Go With the Flow

Understanding dragonfly aerodynamics, how air flows around the bug, will give him a good start. So, Michael runs lots of experiments. He tests his mini-plane wing designs in wind and water tunnels to see how air and water flows around them. Computerized sensors make measurements and Michael interprets all the information. "I always liked using my hands, doing things that are visual," he says.

MICHAEL OL
Air Force Research Laboratory

From Dragonfly to Airplane

Michael Ol studies airplanes: how fast, how far, and how high they can fly. He also experiments with miniature flying machines that don't need people to fly them. Tiny planes are a big challenge. "We know how big planes fly, but when we try to make them really small, they don't fly very well," Michael tells Sally Ride Science.

Teeny Experts

Not all of Michael's designs come from scratch—nature also offers inspiration. Once, his colleague brought a dragonfly into the lab. This was a "flying machine" that they could try to imitate. Dragonflies are aerial acrobats—they can fly backwards, zip around at 65 kilometers (35 miles) per hour, and then stop on a dime. They can even hover in one place. Michael is researching ways to help engineers translate these moves into airplane designs.

An aerodynamicist studies how air moves around airplanes, cars, and other objects. Michael designs airplanes. Other **aerodynamicists**

* build racecars.
* use computers to model airplanes.
* study how to make hot air balloons fly higher and faster.
* design road bikes.

Imitate and Simulate

Michael looked at a dragonfly for inspiration. If you were designing an airplane, what living things would you try to imitate?

Natural Fliers

Can you finish Michael's quote?

"In addition to insects, b _ _ _ _ and b _ _ _ have been very successful 'miniature airplanes' for millions of years."

Test Flights

Try making several paper airplanes, with different features. Record how differently each flies. Make up your own features to change or use these.

	Heavy weight paper	Light weight paper	Broad wings	Narrow wings	Add weight toward front	Add flaps in wings (use folds or tears)
Changes in flight						
Changes in flight						
Changes in flight						

"We should definitely explore Mars together as a world."

DAVA NEWMAN
Massachusetts Institute of Technology

Futuristic Fashions

"We're designing a Martian spacesuit," Dava Newman tells Sally Ride Science. And unlike the bulky Apollo moonsuits, these will be thin, flexible, and tight—almost a second skin. Slick! But before astronauts make it to Mars, they'll be flying for months, which is why Dava also studies how people adjust to weightlessness.

Step by Step

Dava calls the spacesuit her favorite, but also her "craziest," project. A more down-to-earth project: robotic ankle braces for certain stroke victims. Dava studies how people move—in space or at home—and engineers ways to help them. "You get pretty emotional when you see someone walk normally again," she says.

Bodies and Machines

At her Montana high school, Dava was a ski racer. At college, she played basketball big-time. She says that sports steered her toward biomedical engineering. "It really brought together my technological side as well as my enthusiasm for sports."

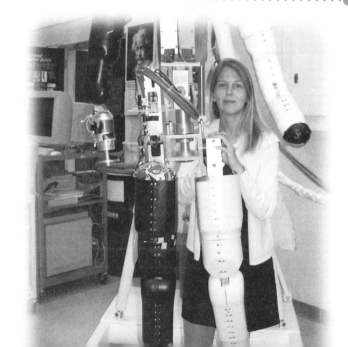

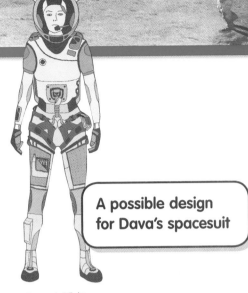

An aerospace biomedical engineer makes biology and technology work together in space and on airplanes. Dava studies how people's bodies move in low gravity or weightlessness. Other **aerospace biomedical engineers**

* design advanced life support systems.

* study bone loss from weightlessness.

* find new ways for people to interact with machines.

* invent medical devices to treat sick astronauts.

A possible design for Dava's spacesuit

Your Own Style

Imagine you're trekking the Martian terrain. What does your spacesuit look like? What features does it have? Sketch your idea on a sheet of paper.

What Would U Do?

While in space, astronauts have done four of Dava's experiments. If you could design an experiment for space, what would it be?

_____

_____

_____

Is It 4 U?

What parts of Dava's job would you like?

❑ Teaching

❑ Creating spacesuits on computers

❑ Building models with your hands

❑ Testing people's bodies as they jump around your lab

❑ Helping people with disabilities

Sports and Space

What would be your favorite sport to play in space? (And don't say water polo!) Would you have to change any rules?

_____

_____

_____

_____

Ephrahim Garcia
Cornell University

Morphing Planes

Growing up, Ephrahim Garcia liked learning about space, science, and new technology. "My dad and I would talk about science and technology and what is possible as a civilization," he tells Sally Ride Science. "I was fascinated by how we went from the horse to the Wright Brothers Flyer to a 747." What's next? Ephrahim's working on the answer to that question: airplanes that can morph, or change shape, in midair.

Nature's Solutions

"Nobody has changed the construction of an airplane much in 100 years," says Ephrahim. He's trying to learn the fundamentals of shape-changing by testing a nine-foot model in a wind tunnel. He's also studying how birds do it. "Sometimes nature's solutions are better than human-made ones," he says.

"We can learn from nature and incorporate natural features into human-made machines to make them work better."

Extreme Makeover

While working for the military, Ephrahim started to think about how useful it would be if planes could change shape. He envisioned planes that could morph their wings to zoom through narrow spaces, or tuck their tails under their wings to make quick landings like birds do.

NASA is planning a flexible airplane for the future. This is a drawing of their "Morphing Airplane."

An aerospace engineer

designs, builds and tests aircraft and spacecraft. Ephrahim uses his skills to develop new types of flexible aircraft. Other **aerospace engineers**

✳ study how the flow of air around a moving aircraft affects its flight.

✳ identify and fix problems in the design of an airplane.

✳ design and build rockets, fighter jets and helicopters.

Who Do U Talk 2?

Ephrahim loved science classes in high school. But he didn't know how to become a scientist until a physics teacher recommended that he study engineering in college. Who do you talk to about your future goals?

Transportation Time Line

As a boy, Ephrahim was intrigued by how transportation changed over the years. Arrange these inventions in order by date, with the oldest invention as number one.

___ Apollo moon landers

___ Horse and buggy

___ Wright Brothers Flyer

___ Space Shuttle

___ The Model T

___ Mars rovers

Mother Nature, Engineer

Nature has inspired many biologically-based designs. Unscramble the words below to see which creatures we've gotten some ideas from.

1. Bird SEAKB _ _ _ _ _ led to the invention of tweezers.

2. Rat SKIERSHW _ _ _ _ _ _ _ _ have led to the development of better sensors.

3. BSRUR _ _ _ _ _ that cling to dog fur inspired the invention of Velcro.

4. DIBR _ _ _ _ wings and tails are inspiring new aircraft designs.

Want to check your answers? Check 'Em Out on page 32.

JANICE VOSS
NASA Ames Research Center

Hi, Neighbor!

Janice Voss has circled our planet on five Space Shuttle missions. Now she's reaching much farther out in space, but without leaving Earth. How? She's the Science Director for the *Kepler* spacecraft. After the craft launches, it will spend several years closely monitoring 100,000 stars in our cosmic neighborhood. The goal: to find as many Earth-like planets around these stars as possible.

Science Non-Fiction

Sounds sci-fi, right? No surprise. When Janice was little, the fantasy novel *A Wrinkle in Time* "started me on the science fiction path," she says. "The more I touched, the more I liked." Janice began reading science *non-fiction* too, and soon she knew she had to go into space herself. In graduate school, Janice studied rocket-fuel mixtures and space station structural stability. Then one day she got her call from NASA.

Life Goes On

"Flying in space was great," Janice tells Sally Ride Science. "I like the environment, it's really fun. But what I really enjoyed was the people and the team and the fun of discovering new stuff. Well, I'm still doing that here."

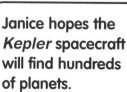

Janice hopes the *Kepler* spacecraft will find hundreds of planets.

An astronaut travels into space to explore our world and what lies beyond. Astronauts have different backgrounds, including aviation, engineering, science, and teaching. Their different skills are important in space. Janice conducted experiments on the Space Shuttle. She grew crystals, played with fire, and mapped Earth in three dimensions. Other **astronauts**

* release satellites into space.
* study Earth's weather and geology from above.
* build the International Space Station.

Tee Hee

Q. Where do astronauts leave their spaceships?

A. At the parking "meteor"!

Did U Know?

Only about 450 people have ever traveled into space. Forty of them have been women.

Astronaut Firsts

Match the astronaut (or cosmonaut, which is what Russians call their space explorers) with what she accomplished in space. We did one for you.

1) Shannon Lucid   **a)** First woman in space

2) Mae Carol Jemison   **b)** First American woman in space

3) Eileen Collins   **c)** First Hispanic woman in space

4) Sally Ride   **d)** Woman who's spent most time in space

5) Ellen Ochoa   **e)** First African-American woman in space

6) Valentina Tereshkova   **f)** First woman Space Shuttle pilot/commander

Want to check your answers? Check 'Em Out on page 32.

LORENDA WARD

National Transportation Safety Board

Taking Charge

When it comes to aerospace engineering, "most people think of building or flying airplanes," Lorenda Ward tells Sally Ride Science, "but there are those of us out here who actually put them back together." As an Investigator in Charge, Lorenda is one of the first on the scene of big plane crashes, and it's her job to figure out what happened and why.

Stress Junkie

Examining accidents can get stressful, "but it's not a bad stress," Lorenda says. "We stay focused on the fact that we're here to make flying safer for the next group of folks." Plus, she adds, "I like the hands-on aspect. It gets the adrenaline going."

Creative Combo

In an eighth-grade survey, Lorenda had to pick three careers she was interested in. "I picked pilot, reporter, and FBI agent. That's kinda cool, because now I'm kinda doing all three of them."

> "Ever since I was little, I just loved airplanes and space."

> Lorenda investigated the Pentagon plane crash on 9/11.

The FDR (flight data recorder)

The CVR (cockpit voice recorder)

An aviation safety engineer

An aviation safety engineer makes sure that we can fly as safely as possible. Lorenda is in charge of large aircraft accident investigations. Other **aviation safety engineers**

* study wing materials in labs.
* build flight simulators to train pilots.
* program flight software that keeps planes on course.

What Happened?

Match the clues with what they can tell you about a plane crash.

___ **1.** Tapes what the pilots say before the crash

___ **2.** Monitors what the plane is doing before the crash

___ **3.** Might tell if a storm caused the crash

___ **4.** Could show if the plane hit the ground in one piece

a) flight data recorder

b) wreckage distribution

c) cockpit voice recorder

d) weather report

Is It 4 U?

What part of Lorenda's job would you like?

❑ Flying around the world on a moment's notice

❑ Talking to reporters on TV

❑ Piecing together airplane wreckage

❑ Preparing computer simulations of accidents

Woman in Charge

Lorenda is one of only five Investigators in Charge and only the second woman ever. Most aerospace engineers are men. According to Lorenda, "We need to get more women out here!" What percent do you think are women?

a) 10%

b) 25%

c) 40%

Want to check your answers? Check 'Em Out on page 32.

ALEXANDRE BAYEN

University of California, Berkeley

Math to the Rescue

There's good news for busy air traffic controllers and pilots. Alexandre Bayen wants to make their jobs easier. This civil systems engineer is using his math and engineering skills to turn the problem of air traffic congestion into a math problem. He believes that solving it could lead to a warning system that will not only prevent crashes, but will also cut down on airport delays. "Mathematics is a fantastic tool," he tells Sally Ride Science.

Faster, Safer, Better

To create computer tools to help air traffic controllers, Alexandre is coming up with math equations for all the possible flight paths that could lead to a collision between two planes. The information could be programmed into a control center to automatically warn air traffic controllers when planes are in danger. The same system could also make airports more efficient by informing air traffic controllers when it's safe to line up airborne planes for landing. "It's nice to be able to contribute to making things work better," Alexandre says. That adds up.

> "Engineering is really about modeling everyday problems and putting equations behind what you see."

This control center has real people reacting to simulations as they test future technology.

A civil systems engineer

uses math and engineering to analyze complicated systems that are made up of many parts, each affecting the others. Alexandre is working to make air traffic flow better at airports. Other **civil systems engineers**

* improve the flow of highway traffic.
* use electronics to monitor earthquakes.
* work on improving unpiloted airplanes.

About You

As a boy growing up in France, Alexandre loved solving math problems at school. He later realized that math can be used to solve many everyday problems, too. How do you use math in your life?

Is It 4 U?

Alexandre loves his job. What parts of it would you like?

❑ Going into the field to observe air traffic controllers at work

❑ Crunching numbers to come up with solutions to problems

❑ Using your smarts to make an impact on society

❑ Being a mentor to young engineering students

Math is Everywhere

Can you circle the hidden numbers in the sentences below? We did the first one for you.

1. The cross-country trip was so exciting, Matt had fun in every state! (nine)

2. Because of her height, Captain Ellie needed a longer flightsuit.

3. When the plane landed, we all took off our seatbelts.

4. Roberto never gets airsick.

5. Janet won the airplane design contest.

Want to check your answers? Check 'Em Out on page 32.

Big to Small

At Howard University, Aprille studied how big structures, such as space stations, flex and vibrate in orbit. It's like architecture, but for stuff that moves. Then she wrote software programs to control the orbits of smaller satellites. Now she manages the design of the instruments, such as X ray cameras, that go on these cosmic cruisers.

Aprille Ericsson
NASA Goddard Space Flight Center

Help from Far Away

How do satellites orbiting hundreds of kilometers above Earth help us? Ask Aprille Ericsson, who puts some of those satellites into orbit. She's worked on spacecraft that study tropical rainfall, the origins of the Universe, and the effects of solar flares on our planet. "The hardware that I build produces scientific data that allow us to understand the Universe and our environment better and help us in our daily lives and communities," she tells Sally Ride Science.

Puzzling and Questioning

Aprille grew up in the projects in Brooklyn. There her mom and grandfathers (both engineers) prodded her to use her mind—and her hands. "Picking apart and looking at things around you, asking questions, and then trying to put the puzzles together were all important skills that I learned as a kid. I've been able to apply them all in my career."

Aprille reviews the construction and testing of a NASA satellite.

A mechanical engineer

designs, builds, and tests machines and structures. Aprille manages the teams of scientists and engineers who build instruments for satellites. Other **mechanical engineers**

✴ build rovers that explore planets.

✴ make cars safer in crashes.

✴ test models of bridges and skyscrapers.

✴ use computer-aided design (CAD) software.

Did U Know?

The Russians launched *Sputnik 1,* the world's first artificial satellite, into orbit on October 4, 1957. *Sputnik* means "satellite" in Russian.

Satellites' Light

Satellites can orbit hundreds of kilometers above Earth, but are easy to see at night, even without a telescope or binoculars. Here's how.

1. Pick a night when there's no Moon.

2. Find someplace far from artificial lights, beginning an hour or two after sunset.

3. Look up and search for a bright object that moves steadily and slowly across the sky.

You've just seen your first satellite! Remember, shooting stars move quickly, and airplanes have blinking lights. Satellites look like stars, but they move. The light you see is the reflection of the Sun's rays.

Out of Sight, Out of Mind?

We rely on satellites every day. What kind of satellites would you need if you wanted to

1) know if it's going to be cloudy tomorrow?

2) watch television?

3) phone someone in another country?

4) see recent pictures of nearby planets?

5) get directions through GPS?

a) Communications satellites

b) Navigation satellites

c) Solar system observation satellites

d) Broadcast satellites

e) Weather satellites

Want to check your answers? Check 'Em Out on page 32.

VICTORIA COVERSTONE
University of Illinois at Urbana-Champaign

Mission Critical

Imagine an asteroid headed straight for Earth. Unstopped, it will hit us. We have ten years to prepare. What should we do? What's the asteroid made of? Can we blow it up? Can we redirect it? That's what Victoria Coverstone asked her college students last year. They had to design spacecraft, instruments, and strategies that could save our planet.

Fresh Eyes

Victoria is fascinated by her fancy equations, but she says she most enjoys working with her students. "They're bright, they're full of energy, and they're passionate about where they see that our society could go," she says. "It keeps you fresh."

The Future of Flight

In her own research, Victoria programs computers to figure out the best paths for spacecraft to take on long trips. And she specializes in the paths of future "low-thrust" spacecraft, such as those that use solar sails, which will be pushed by sunlight alone. That requires lots of difficult math, because these spacecraft will need to adjust their paths constantly along the journey.

"Math is a building block that allows you to go into many different careers."

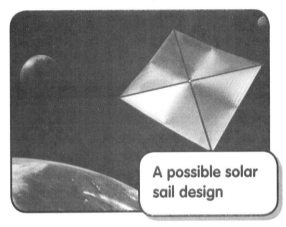

A mission designer plans a space mission that can include one or more spacecraft. Victoria designs flight paths for low-thrust spacecraft. Other **mission designers**

✴ select destinations.

✴ design spacecraft.

✴ choose instruments and experiments to put in spacecraft.

A possible solar sail design

Build It!

Want to build a scale model of a real solar sail? Check out *http://spacecraftkits.com/cosmos1/index.html*

Your Turn

If you could plan a mission to any place in our solar system, where would you want to explore? What would you send there?

Propulsion Possibilities

Across

5. Someday we may send a light sail to another star. It would be hundreds of times the size of a _____ field and pushed by a laser from Earth.

Down

1. Solar sails will be pushed by particles of light called _____.

2. Some low-thrust spacecraft will be powered by _____ reactors.

3. Once in space, most spacecraft use the _____ of planets and moons to change direction.

4. Some low-thrust spacecraft will be powered by _____ panels.

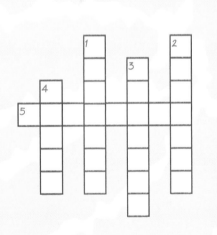

Want to check your answers? Check 'Em Out on page 32.

PENINA "PENNY" AXELRAD

University of Colorado at Boulder

Think Globally

As a young girl, Penny Axelrad thought she wanted to become an astronaut. Then she found an exciting way to work in space without going there. She started working with the Global Positioning System (GPS) to track the planned International Space Station. Penny was hooked! "GPS kept changing, and I kept learning new things, so I've stayed in this field for more than 20 years now," she tells Sally Ride Science.

What's GPS?

GPS is a worldwide navigation system made up of satellites orbiting our planet. They send radio signals to receivers on the ground and can pinpoint any place on Earth. If your family's car has a GPS receiver, the signals can show you where you are on a map on a dashboard computer screen. Penny's job is to find the best way to use GPS navigation satellites to track other satellites, such as those that photograph Earth's surface.

Problem Solver

Penny also enjoys teaching at the University of Colorado. "If a student doesn't know how to do something, I help her solve the problem by breaking it down to solvable pieces." Does that mean Penny helps her students *navigate* their way to answers?

A navigation engineer

uses technology to determine the exact location of people and objects. Penny designs ways to use GPS to track science satellites. Other **navigation engineers**

* design cell phones that can tell you where you are.
* build hand-held computers to guide the blind.
* improve safety of air traffic or aircraft landing systems.
* develop systems to track the migration of animals.

Lost and Found

You could use GPS in many different ways. Name some situations in which it might come in handy.

_____

_____

_____

Treasure Hunt

If you don't have a GPS receiver, check "Lower-Tech" to the right for some handy tools you can use for a navigation system. Then, engineer your own treasure hunt: hide something and create some navigation clues to guide someone to it.

Lower-Tech

Unscramble the letters below and find old-fashioned ways of navigating. Which ones are we still using today?

1. Piece of paper with landmarks to help you find your way

PMA _____

2. Shining point in the sky that sailors used to cross the ocean

NOTHR SART _____

3. Its arrow points north

MAPSCOS _____

Want to check your answers? Check 'Em Out on page 32.

Christopher Wickens

University of Illinois at Urbana-Champaign (retired)

A Better Outlook?

Imagine flying an airplane through thick clouds. It would help if you could see the skies ahead on a screen in front of you, right? If Christopher Wickens has his way, someday soon airplanes will have smart screens like these.

Better Designs

Chris realized that pilots might have an easier time if their equipment were less confusing, especially the rows of clock-like instrument gauges in cockpits. He and his colleagues began designing and testing different displays. They've come up with ones that have the same information, but in a way the brain can better digest. Among those being reviewed: screens that show images of the ground below (helpful when it's cloudy), 3-D maps of Earth, and visuals that guide pilots along their flight paths. On top of these, pilots could add visuals showing their altitude, airspeed, or fuel levels. Will these designs take off? Roger that.

> "We're seeing the results of our research and how these cockpit displays will be built in the next generation."

Brains in Flight

Chris is a research psychologist who became curious in college about how the brain sorts out information. "I was just fascinated by how people understand each other and how the world works," he says. He was particularly impressed by pilots, whose busy brains juggle many tasks at once.

> Chris isn't a pilot but he does reach high altitudes. An avid mountain climber, he's scaled more than 56 peaks above 4,000 meters (14,000 feet)!

A psychologist is trained in human behavior and how the mind works. Chris studies how pilots fly so that better equipment can be designed. Other **psychologists**

* study how humans learn and what methods might help them.
* conduct experiments to see how machines, such as computers, can be used to assist people.
* help people to cope with accidents, stress, or family problems.

Mental Juggling

Pilots have to handle many responsibilities at once. You do, too. List some ways that you make your brain do some mental juggling. Here are some common examples.

I do homework while watching television.

I talk on a cell phone while shopping.

_____

_____

_____

Earn Your Wings

Find and circle some of the tasks a pilot has to do on the job.

CHECK WEATHER   COMMUNICATE
CRUISE   FLY   LAND
SCAN THE SKIES   TAKE OFF

```
S W C G M M M P H X B T
R E H T A E W K C E H C
U T I X U P C F T C I F
K A K K N A K L L P F K
Q C S D S A K Y Y O H L
R I Q R Z E M N E R J F
R N G Z S L H K L P C X
I U O M K H A T T E U Y
K M Q O O T C N N A Y V
C M C R U I S E D A V K
D O N R W A D I U V C D
D C Z S M N X V Z Y F S
```

About You

Chris loved geology as a kid but got hooked on psychology in college. What subjects do you like?

_____   _____

_____   _____

What subjects do you think might interest you in the future?

_____   _____

_____   _____

Want to check your answers? Check 'Em Out on page 32.

"I've learned a lot about how spacecraft work. I'm becoming somewhat of a rocket scientist. . . ."

JANANDA HILL

Northrop Grumman Space Technology

No Do-Overs!

In space, you don't get a second chance. If you've built an advanced satellite, you'd better make sure before launch that it works right. There's no 1-800-REPAIRS up there. That's why Jananda Hill's job—designing software used to test circuit boards for spacecraft—is so crucial to mission success.

Tough Love

Space is a harsh place, so these are not your average VCR circuit boards. To make sure they're space-worthy, engineers must shake, bake, freeze, squeeze, and basically abuse these boards while Jananda's software looks for glitches. They even run them in vacuum chambers and zap them with radiation.

Fun for Our Benefit

Some of the boards will help analyze our environment from orbit, some will gaze into space, and—shhhh!— some are strictly top secret. "It's a lot of fun," Jananda tells Sally Ride Science. "When you see a project you're working on show up on CNN, it makes you feel like you're really doing something important that's contributing to the scientific community, to the nation, and to the world."

A circuit board holds electronic parts and wires together. Check out the one Jananda is holding.

A software engineer

writes programs for computers. Jananda designs software that tests circuit boards for satellites and space probes. Other **software engineers**

✳ create programming languages to control robots.

✳ make computer graphics more realistic.

✳ help you download music faster.

✳ cram more features into your cell phone.

Countless Code

Software programs are written in a language called computer code. Your home computer contains tens of millions of lines of code!

Test Yourself

Jananda's software will test circuit boards for several projects.

___ **1.** The James Webb Space Telescope (above) will replace the _____ Space Telescope.

___ **2.** Two environmental satellites will help forecast the _____.

___ **3.** ASTRO will robotically upgrade and _____ satellites so they last longer.

___ **4.** A military communications satellite will help keep _____ safe in battle.

    a. soldiers   **c.** Hubble
    b. weather   **d.** refuel

Computers R Everywhere

Circuit boards aren't just for computers and satellites. They run things all around you. Match the descriptions to the machines.

1) Plays your favorite flicks   **a)** Microwave oven

2) Keeps you groovin' as you're movin'   **b)** Car

3) Fixes feasts fast   **c)** DVD player

4) Rolls around town   **d)** Wristwatch

5) Tells time in a jiffy   **e)** iPod

Want to check your answers? Check 'Em Out on page 32.

ROGER LAUNIUS

Smithsonian National Air and Space Museum

Telling Stories

Roger Launius likes to tell stories about the past. After all, he is a historian. He especially likes stories about the history of space exploration. "I really enjoy hunting for historical documents, then making sense of the past," Roger tells Sally Ride Science. He likes to compare old 1950s illustrations of the Moon's surface with more recent photographs—we've learned a lot. He's also interested in how space flight has become part of our everyday lives—there was even an astronaut in the MTV logo!

Predicting the Future

Roger has written a lot of books. His favorite? The one about the first 100 years of space flight. Wait a minute—we've only been traveling in space for the last 50 years. Roger combined his knowledge of the past with his imagination and predicted the future of space travel.

> "When creating a museum exhibit, we ask: 'What story do we want to tell?'"

Curious Questions

Lots of people ask Roger questions. Kids often want to know about explorers, "Who was the first person on the Moon?" White House officials, members of Congress, and reporters often want research on past space travel. Knowing history helps them plan, "How can we use our last trip to the Moon to prepare for future trips?" Good question.

> Roger shows two friends around the National Air and Space Museum.

A historian investigates the past. Roger studies the history of space exploration. He also writes books and creates museum exhibits. Other **historians**

* collect and catalog artifacts.
* work in museums or libraries.
* teach college history courses.

Making History

It's the year 2100. You're a space historian at a museum. Which exhibit about the past would you create?

1. The first elevator to space

2. The first Mars colony

3. Life discovered on another planet

4. Your idea _____.

Your Story

Think about the history of your life. How would you divide it up? What were some of the big events that happened? Can you use what you've learned about your life to plan your future?

_____

_____

All in a Day's Work

In Roger's job, he deals with all of these. Can you find and circle them?

ARTIFACTS   FUTURE   HISTORY
MUSEUM   QUESTIONS   TEACHING
WRITING

```
H M Z K A N E H S L O N
I F U T A Z F T K T Z T
S G C E E F C I W T V R
T J R W S A K Z Q Q W I
O V T X F U C B N R D I
R F T I H M M H I C L U
Y U T Q U E S T I O N S
E R M B X I I W R N F B
A Q P W Z N O Z P P G S
W E H L G E R U T U F M
B Q Q O C W B A R S F U
Z I D Z Q P S K O S Z X
```

Want to check your answers? Check 'Em Out on page 32.

About Me...

My name is _____.

I'm in grade _____ at _____ school.

I like learning about
- ❏ Rockets
- ❏ Airplanes
- ❏ Satellites
- ❏ Astronauts
- ❏ Space stations
- ❏ Spacesuits

(other) _____

If I could go to space, I would visit
- ❏ A space station
- ❏ The Moon
- ❏ Another planet
- ❏ Another planet's moon
- ❏ A comet
- ❏ Another solar system

(other) _____

I would like to work with
- ❏ Computers
- ❏ Wind tunnels
- ❏ Rocket engines
- ❏ Space vehicles
- ❏ Students
- ❏ Pilots

(other) _____

I like
- ❏ Doing experiments
- ❏ Drawing pictures
- ❏ Building things
- ❏ Asking questions
- ❏ Working with people
- ❏ Thinking of inventions

(other) _____

★ My best subjects in school are _____

_____

★ I would rather (a) fly (b) design airplanes and
rockets, because _____

_____

★ I think aerospace is important because _____

_____

★ I think the best part of living in space would be _____

_____

★ I think the worst part of living in space would be _____

_____

★ I wish airplanes could _____

_____

★ Someone who really inspires me or encourages me is

_____ because_____

★ If I could invite someone to visit my school, I would invite
_____

I would invite her or him because _____

_____

★ My dream job would be _____

CHECK 'EM OUT: Answers

AERODYNAMICIST, page 7

Natural Fliers
birds, bats

AEROSPACE ENGINEER, page 11

Mother Nature, Engineer
1. beaks 2. whiskers 3. burrs 4. bird

Transportation Time Line
4, 1, 2, 5, 3, 6

ASTRONAUT, page 13

Astronaut Firsts
Shannon Lucid: Woman who's spent most time in space
Mae Carol Jemison: First African-American woman in space
Eileen Collins: First woman Space Shuttle pilot/comman der
Sally Ride: First American woman in space
Ellen Ochoa: First Hispanic woman in space
Valentina Tereshkova: First woman in space

AVIATION SAFETY ENGINEER, page 15

What Happened?
1. c 2. a 3. d 4. b

Woman in Charge
Only 10% of aerospace engineers are women.

CIVIL SYSTEMS ENGINEER, page 17

Math is Everywhere
fun in every
Height
off our
Roberto never
Janet won

MECHANICAL ENGINEER, page 19

Out of Sight, Out of Mind?
Communications satellites: phone someone in another country
Navigation satellites: get directions through GPS
Solar system observation satellites: see recent pictures of nearby planets
Broadcast satellites: watch television
Weather satellites: know if it's going to be cloudy tomorrow

MISSION DESIGNER, page 21

Propulsion Possibilities
Across
5. football
Down
1. photons
2. nuclear
3. gravity
4. solar

NAVIGATION ENGINEER, page 23

Lower-Tech
1. map 2. North Star 3. compass

PSYCHOLOGIST, page 25

Earn Your Wings

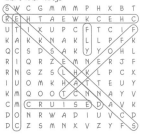

SOFTWARE ENGINEER, page 27

Computers R Everywhere
Plays your favorite flicks: DVD player
Keeps you groovin' as you're movin': iPod
Fixes feasts fast: microwave
Rolls around town: car
Tells time in a jiffy: wristwatch

Test Yourself
c, b, d, a

SPACE HISTORIAN , page 29

All in a Day's Work